Facts About the

Western Diamondback Rattlesnake

By Lisa Strattin

© 2016 Lisa Strattin

Revised © 2019

Facts for Kids Picture Books by Lisa Strattin

Harlequin Macaw, Vol 34

Downy Woodpecker, Vol 37

Frilled Lizard, Vol 39

Purple Finch, Vol 48

Poison Dart Frogs, Vol 50

Giant Otter, Vol 57

Hornbill, Vol 67

Dwarf Lemur, Vol 73

Giant Squirrel, Vol 76

Star Tortoise, Vol 79

Sign Up for New Release Emails Here

http://LisaStrattin.com/subscribe-here

Monthly Surprise Box

http://KidCraftsByLisa.com

All information in this book has been carefully researched and checked for factual accuracy. However, the author and publisher makes no warranty, express or implied, that the information contained herein is appropriate for every individual, situation or purpose and assume no responsibility for errors or omissions. The reader assumes the risk and full responsibility for all actions, and the author will not be held responsible for any loss or damage, whether consequential, incidental, special or otherwise, that may result from the information presented in this book.

All images are free for use or purchased from stock photo sites for commercial use.

Some coloring pages might be of the general species due to lack of available images.

I have relied on my own observations as well as many different sources for this book and I have done my best to check facts and give credit where it is due. In the event that any material is used without proper permission, please contact me so that the oversight can be corrected.

Contents

INTRODUCTION

The western diamondback rattlesnake is one of the longest snakes in North America, and is also a thick-bodied animal. Its range includes much of the southwestern United States and Mexico, from the coasts to the mountains.

As with other rattlesnakes, the western diamondback has a distinctive rattle on the end of its tail that it shakes when it feels threatened.

CHARACTERISTICS

Rattlesnakes tend to be solitary animals, though in the winter they sometimes hibernate in large groups.

Like other reptiles, they are "ectothermic." This means that, unlike mammals that can produce their own body heat to keep warm, reptiles need an outside source of heat to stay alive. In the summer, rattlesnakes and other reptiles use the sun's heat, and can often be seen basking on warm rocks, or even in the middle of roads, in order to bring their body temperature up high enough for them to hunt for food.

In the winter, many snakes, including western diamondbacks, find caves or deep cracks in large rocks in which to hibernate.

APPEARANCE

As its name implies, the western diamondback has diamond-shaped patterns along its back and face. Over most of its body, its patterns vary in color, with shades of brown and gray and bands that are sometimes pink, white, or yellow, depending on its environment. These changing patterns and colors help it blend in with the dead leaves and rocks, making it hard to see.

On its tail near its rattle are black and white stripes, markings that are distinctly different from the rest of its body.

LIFE STAGES

Rattlesnakes are reptiles. While most reptiles lay eggs, much like birds, western diamondbacks are "ovoviviparous," which means that the babies actually break through their shell just before their mother gives birth. This means that these rattlesnakes are born live, in a manner similar to the way mammals are born.

Gestation, the time in which a baby or an egg is in its mother's womb, lasts between six and seven months, and a brood can be of between one- or two-dozen snakes, each nearly a foot in length. From the moment of their birth, diamondbacks are able to deliver a venomous bite. Mother diamondbacks will stay with their young often for several hours, and sometimes for as long as a day, before the young leave. Unlike mammals, snakes are unable to nurse their young, and so even at just a day old, the baby snakes are already able to hunt for their own food.

At three years, a rattlesnake is considered to be a mature adult.

Like other reptiles and amphibians, as diamondback rattlesnakes grow, their scaly skin does not grow with them, but must be shed periodically because it no longer fits; it's not uncommon to find shed snake skins lying on the ground near their dens. With each shedding, a segment is added to the rattlesnake's rattle, which makes some people think that a rattlesnake's age can be measured by the number of rattles in its tail. But this isn't true. Not only do snakes not always shed once a year, but they also sometimes lose parts of their rattles!

A rattlesnake's rattle is made out of keratin; other things made out of keratin include a person's hair, fingernails, and a snake's scales. On a snake's rattle, segments of hard keratin are fitted loosely inside each other, and the snake produces its distinctive sound by raising its tail and shaking it. Animals and people who hear this sound know that the rattlesnake isn't happy, and is ready to strike.

LIFE SPAN

In captivity, western diamondbacks have been known to live for as long as twenty years. In the wild, however, where they have to find their own food and face the threats of starvation, dehydration, and other predators, they probably don't live nearly so long.

SIZE

This is one of the largest venomous snakes in the United States, getting as long as 7 feet, or nearly as tall as the ceiling in some rooms, though they more often grow to only be about 4 feet long, or only a little taller than most second graders.

HABITAT

Western diamondbacks live across the southwestern United States, including Arizona, Texas, Oklahoma, and southern California, and their range extends into the northern half of Mexico.

Within their range of the Southwest, they can be found living from below sea level to more than a mile up into the mountains, in plains and forests that see frequent rain and in very dry deserts. They can swim across rivers, have even been found on some of the coastal islands, and can climb trees. They are able to live in many different environments and get around almost anywhere!

DIET

Rattlesnakes are carnivores, which means they eat meat, and don't eat fruits or vegetables. Their favorite prey includes such things as mice, rabbits, birds (when they can catch them,) lizards, and other small animals.

Like other venomous snakes, a rattlesnake will bite its prey to inject it with venom, and then wait until the animal becomes so sick that it can no longer move, before swallowing it whole.

Western diamondbacks can regularly go for as long as five months between meals, and have been known to not eat for as long as two years.

FRIENDS AND ENEMIES

While diamondbacks have many neighbors, they have very few friends. While they feed on the small animals that live around them, other, larger animals, such as eagles, hawks, roadrunners, coyotes, and foxes, hunt them.

Even large, herbivorous animals, animals that are neither the diamondback's predator nor prey, such as deer, cows, and horses, see the diamondback as a threat to their young, and often try to step on the snake in order to chase it away or even kill it.

SUITABILITY AS PETS

While many reptiles make wonderful pets, the bite of a rattlesnake is extremely poisonous, and so they are only safely handled by experts, with the right equipment (like very, very long poles and thick gloves and boots.) In captivity, such as at a zoo or reptile sanctuary habitat, they will be fed in such a way that their handlers don't have to have direct contact with them.

A western diamondback rattlesnake is not a good choice for a pet for most people.

COLOR ME

COLOR ME

COLOR ME

COLOR ME

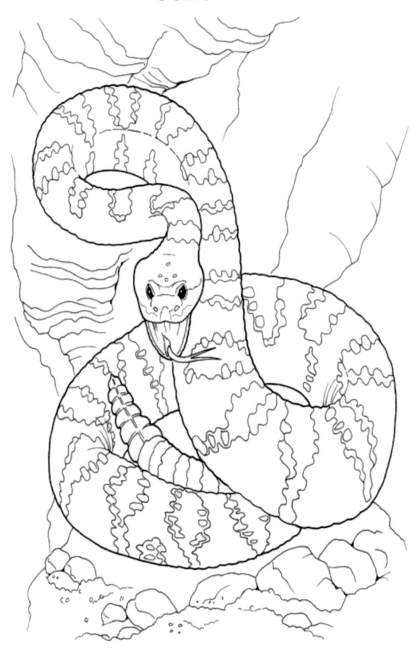

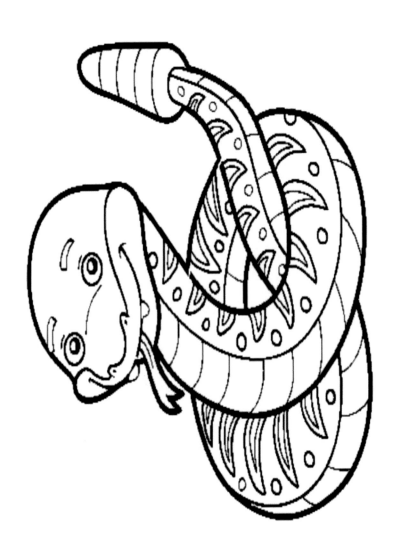

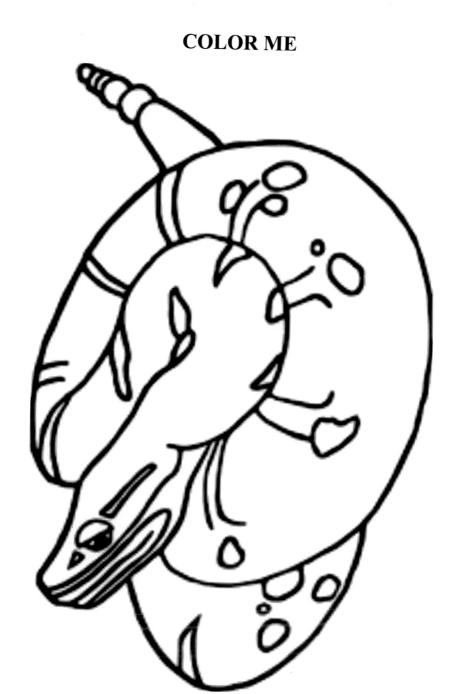

Please leave me a review here:

http://lisastrattin.com/Review-Vol-133

For more Kindle Downloads Visit Lisa Strattin Author Page on Amazon Author Central

http://amazon.com/author/lisastrattin

To see upcoming titles, visit my website at LisaStrattin.com– all books available on kindle!

http://lisastrattin.com

PLUSH RATTLER

You can get one by copying and pasting this link into your browser:

http://lisastrattin.com/plushrattler

MONTHLY SURPRISE BOX

Get yours by copying and pasting this link into your browser

http://KidCraftsByLisa.com

Made in the USA
San Bernardino, CA
30 January 2020